Larry

the Chief Mouser

and other official cats

Important Dates

*c.*8,000 BCE	Cats are first domesticated by people in the Middle East.
3,000–300 BCE	Egyptians worship the cat god Bast, representing fertility, motherhood and protection.
1397	Dick Whittington is elected Lord Mayor of London, possibly with his cat.
1515	Cardinal Wolsey, cat lover, becomes England's Lord Chancellor.
1633	William Laud, known for his cat-fancying, becomes Archbishop of Canterbury.
1830	Lord Palmerston is appointed Foreign Secretary.
1868	William Ewart Gladstone is elected Prime Minister for the first time.
1868	The first official Post Office cat is appointed in London.
1902	Earliest known record of an official cat at the Admiralty.
1924	Ramsay MacDonald becomes the first Labour Prime Minister; he is elected again in 1929.
1929–46	**Peter** serves as the Home Office's first official cat.
1935–37	Stanley Baldwin is Prime Minister.
*c.*1936–42	**Jumbo** – War Cabinet Mouse Exterminator – joins the Cabinet Office.
1937–40	Neville Chamberlain serves as Prime Minister.
1940	Winston Churchill becomes Prime Minister and moves into Downing Street with his cat **Nelson**.
1945–51	Clement Attlee serves as Prime Minister and creates the NHS.
1947–64	The Home Office appoints **Peter II** as their official cat, but he is quickly replaced by **Peter III**.
1949	**Simon**, a Royal Navy cat hero, wins the Dickin Medal.
1951–55	Winston Churchill completes his second term as Prime Minister.
1964–*c.*1970	**Peta** serves as the Home Office cat. Harold Wilson becomes Prime Minister.
1970–74	Ted Heath is Prime Minister.
1973–86	**Wilberforce** serves under PMs Heath, Wilson, Callaghan and Thatcher.
1989–97	**Humphrey** serves as Downing Street's Chief Mouser under PMs Thatcher, Major and (briefly) Blair.
2010	David Cameron becomes Prime Minister after Gordon Brown loses the General Election.
15 February 2011	**Larry** is appointed as first official Chief Mouser to the Cabinet Office.
13 April 2016	**Palmerston** is appointed Chief Mouser to the Foreign Office.
28 June 2016	**Gladstone** is appointed as Mouser to the Treasury.
13 July 2016	Theresa May becomes Prime Minister, and quickly guarantees Larry's safety.
9 December 2017	**Evie** and **Ossie** are appointed as Mousers to the Cabinet Office.

Introduction

Since human societies began to develop agriculture around 10,000 years ago, there has been a shadowy group watching over us, manipulating us. To begin with it was a casual, working relationship – we humans wanted to store grain, which attracted rodents, so we entered into a partnership with these willing pest controllers.

Things changed, though, and the influence of these slinking rat-catchers slowly grew; the Ancient Egyptians venerated them, even elevated them to the status of gods, and today we indulge them ever more with titbits and special beds. They are even allowed to walk through the corridors of power at the very heart of Whitehall, eavesdropping on the conversations of Cabinet Ministers.

Cats. There are over 600 million domestic cats in the world, spread across every continent. Valued initially for their skill at catching vermin, we also value them for their companionship and affection (if they're in the mood for those).

For many years the British government has 'employed' cats as mousers, tasked with controlling Whitehall's rodent population. However, files held at The National Archives show that these government moggies were not purely functional, but captured the hearts of the civil servants and politicians around them. This is their story.

Larry prepares for the royal wedding of Prince William and Catherine Middleton.

Larry, Chief Mouser to the Cabinet Office

In 2011 Number 10 Downing Street, the very heart of government, was plagued by unwanted intruders brazen enough to appear in the Prime Minister's private office.

Downing Street had a rodent problem: rats had been spotted outside; and the interior was overrun with mice. A specialist was needed, so the Prime Minister acquired a cat.

On 15 February 2011, the new Chief Mouser to the Cabinet Office was revealed to the world. Larry, a four-year-old brown-and-white tabby, was adopted from Battersea Cats Home and he quickly captured the nation's heart.

Larry is the first cat to officially hold the title of Chief Mouser to the Cabinet Office, although many government departments have had official cats in the past. Unlike many of his less prestigiously titled predecessors, Larry does not receive a 'salary' from the taxpayer; instead the cost of his food and upkeep are happily paid for by Downing Street staff who, as former Prime Minister David Cameron told Parliament, 'love him very much'.

Larry's ascension to the top of the feline tree (let's hope he doesn't get stuck) was credited to his having excellent mousing skills. Number 10 told the press that Larry had 'a high chase-drive and hunting instinct'.

However, Larry has not taken to his role quite as well as expected. He didn't catch a mouse until two months after his appointment, seemingly preferring

Larry takes a nap after arriving at 10 Downing Street in February 2011.

Larry meets US President Barack Obama.

to catnap rather than catch mice.

Larry has also clashed with Freya, former Chancellor George Osborne's cat, who was reported to be a more effective and gregarious mouser. Frequently straying from home, Freya left Westminster in 2014, possibly because of Larry's animosity. The Westminster rumour mill suggested Larry might be dismissed from his post.

Larry is seemingly unsackable, though. Number 10 has always defended him, saying that Larry 'brings a lot of pleasure to a lot of people'. He receives gifts from his adoring public almost daily.

2016 was a tumultuous year in British politics, but Larry has survived and thrived. Incoming Prime Minister Theresa May was quick to say she had no intention to 'reshuffle' the Chief Mouser.

According to Larry's staff profile on Number 10's website, his duties remain much the same, including 'testing antique furniture for napping quality'. Larry's mission to rid Downing Street of rodents, however, is still 'in its tactical planning stage'.

Larry and George Osborne's cat Freya in a fight.

Palmerston, Chief Mouser to the Foreign Office

As already stated, Larry is occasionally a lacklustre mouser, but the same cannot be said for Larry's neighbour, the young upstart Chief Mouser to the Foreign Office, Palmerston.

Named after Victorian Foreign Secretary Lord Palmerston, this new moggy was adopted from Battersea Cats Home on 13 April 2016. Lord Palmerston was known for his aggressive foreign policy and Palmerston the cat seems to have emulated this forceful style in his mousing duties, making his first kill on 3 May.

Since then, while Larry has napped, Palmerston has not ceased in his diligence. As of 6 August 2016 he had 20 'confirmed mouse kills', a fact he announced on his official Twitter feed. He has not shirked his diplomatic duties either, regularly receiving delighted foreign dignitaries. He also takes an active part in office life, attending staff meetings (albeit asleep).

Nevertheless, the Foreign Office Mouser has developed a rivalry with his neighbour, facing off with Larry for the honour of being Whitehall's top cat. On 17 July 2016, just days after David Cameron's resignation, Larry and Palmerston were photographed in a brawl. Cats are notoriously territorial, and these two mousers are no exception.

Their rivalry continued apace over the summer of 2016: Larry had to visit the vet, his paw injured in a catfight, while Palmerston seemed to be missing some fur. At one point Palmerston had to be evicted from Number 10, having staged a daring raid on Larry's home territory. The mousers' relationship became so 'catty' that they had to be temporarily separated!

Gladstone, Evie and Ossie

While Larry and Palmerston were distracted by their turf war, several new cats have appeared on the Westminster scene. Gladstone (right – named after Victorian Chancellor and Prime Minister William Ewart Gladstone) assumed the office of Chief Mouser to the Treasury in June 2016.

Another rehomed cat from Battersea, Gladstone is quite the dandy, often affecting to wear a spotted red bowtie. In December 2016 the Cabinet Office adopted mother-and-son team Evie and Ossie from the Celia Hammond Animal Trust. Larry and Palmerston had better watch their backs – there are new cats in town.

Chief Mouser
Palmerston explores
his new surroundings
in the Foreign and
Commonwealth Office in
London, April 2016.

Palmerston arrives from
Battersea Dogs & Cats Home.

Dick Whittington and his loyal cat.

Cats at the Royal Court

Dick Whittington's cat is one of the most enduring characters of British folklore. The real Sir Richard Whittington (c.1354–1423) was a successful merchant and served as Lord Mayor of London four times. However, his folkloric counterpart Dick is far better known. The legend has it that Dick came to the capital in rags and ascended to riches – in no small part due to his faithful cat's astounding abilities as a rat-catcher.

Despite this, historical records show that the centuries between 1200 and 1700 could be a dangerous time for England's mousers. Medieval religious decrees had led to cats being associated with witchcraft. Agnes Waterhouse, the first woman to be executed for witchcraft in 1566, admitted to having a cat, named Satan, as her familiar.

Nevertheless, cats are mostly absent from historical records and it is likely that our ancestors just weren't as interested in cats as we are.

This indifference did not extend to other pets, though. Elizabeth I was certainly fond of the domestic cat's larger cousins. State Papers at The National Archives record her granting salaries to two brothers as 'Keepers of the Lions, Lionesses and Leopards in the Tower of London', part of the Royal Menagerie kept at the Tower from the reign of King John until 1835.

Thomas Cromwell gave Henry VIII civets, monkeys and marmosets, while Anne Boleyn was said to set 'much store by a pretty dog'.

Meanwhile, a pet of Edward Seymour, Duke of Somerset (1500–52), seems to have come a cropper thanks to the feline hunting instinct. In 1539 he reported in a letter to a friend that a bird they had sent him as a present had been 'killed by a cat' (possibly named Sylvester).

Early modern history does indicate a number of cat lovers in the upper echelons of the Church. Cardinal Wolsey, one of Henry VIII's chief advisers, is reported to have brought a cat along to court when he was Lord Chancellor. And Charles I's favourite, Archbishop William Laud, was said to take 'much delight' in his many pet cats.

These two men were not only important churchmen, but leading politicians of their day – proof that cats have been 'at the heart of government' for some time.

Princess Alexandra of Wales with her pet cat.

Downing Street's Other Mousers

Whitehall has had a steady stream of mousers since at least the 19th century, but not all these moggies show up in the official record. Most cats were 'freelance' – expected to feed themselves through mousing and begging. Only when particularly skilled moggies were taken on as 'official cats', entitled to a Treasury-authorised living allowance, do the government mousers leave a paper trail, their stories preserved in records held at The National Archives.

Some mousers have gained their position simply by being a Cabinet minister's pet, but there have been a number of more permanent mousers, too, serving as diligent 'civil servants' while the governments around them rose and fell.

Wilberforce the cat saw four Prime Ministers come and go during his tenure in Downing Street (1973–86). Prime Minister Ted Heath originally authorised Wilberforce's appointment, but he went on to serve the governments of Harold Wilson, James Callaghan and Margaret

Home Office
Aug 6th 1948

Mr. McMullin
please is it possible for the Office Cats food money to be increased, as it is impossible to buy a weeks food for 1/6, since I came to the office on May 29th, I have increased the amount myself by 6d a week, but I cannot continue to do so.
Yours Sincerely
L. Law. (mrs).

Mrs Law requests an increase in the cat allowance, August 1948.

Wilberforce at Downing Street in 1983.

Thatcher. The Iron Lady was so enamoured with her mouser that she brought him a tin of sardines back from a visit to Russia, an honour that many ministers would have given their right arm for.

Wilberforce retired to the country in 1986, and in 1989 a new mouser appeared. Humphrey was a stray black and white cat who was adopted by Downing Street staff.

Humphrey's career spanned from 1989 to 1997 and was not without controversy. In 1995 he was accused of murdering baby robins, but this accusation ultimately proved to be false.

As Tony Blair entered Number 10, Humphrey retired to the countryside home of a civil servant. However, Westminster's cat-watchers were suspicious, fearing Humphrey had been 'murdered' by the supposedly cat-phobic Blairs. Happily, photographic evidence of Humphrey's new rural life was quickly produced.

Gordon Brown was said to be keen to break away from Tony Blair's style of government when he became Prime Minister, so it is perhaps unsurprising that 2007 saw the return of a mouser to Downing Street. Chancellor Alistair Darling moved into Number 11, bringing his cat Sybil with him.

Although officially residing next door, Sybil was granted a free run of Number 10. ('It's quite difficult to confine cats,' a spokesman observed.) Sybil's era of Mew Labour was to be short-lived, though, as Westminster life did not agree with her. In 2009 she returned to the Darlings' family home in Scotland.

Sybil licks her lips in the garden of the Prime Minister's home, September 2007.

Cherie Blair dispells current rumours that she is not a cat lover by posing with Humphrey in the gardens of Number 10 in May 1997.

Churchill's Moggies

Winston Churchill is perhaps the most celebrated of Britons, known for his indefatigable spirit and acerbic wit, amongst other things. He was also extremely fond of felines.

'He loved cats … He always had a cat, if not two,' one of Churchill's secretaries recalled. Accordingly, Churchill made sure when moving in to Number 10 in May 1940, with the imperilled nation's hope resting upon his shoulders as the Second World War raged, to bring his favourite cat, Nelson, with him.

Despite his owner's aristocratic credentials, Nelson was no pedigree. Churchill had seen

Nelson ('the bravest cat I ever knew') chasing a dog out of the Admiralty; impressed by the cat's boldness, Churchill adopted him, naming him after Admiral Nelson.

Nelson's move into Number 10 was bad news for its incumbent cat, who had served departing Prime Minister Neville Chamberlain. The Munich Mouser, as Churchill unkindly nicknamed him, was soon chased off by Nelson.

But Nelson was the PM's personal cat so cannot really stake a claim for the title of Chief Mouser; amongst the 'official' cats of the time, perhaps the

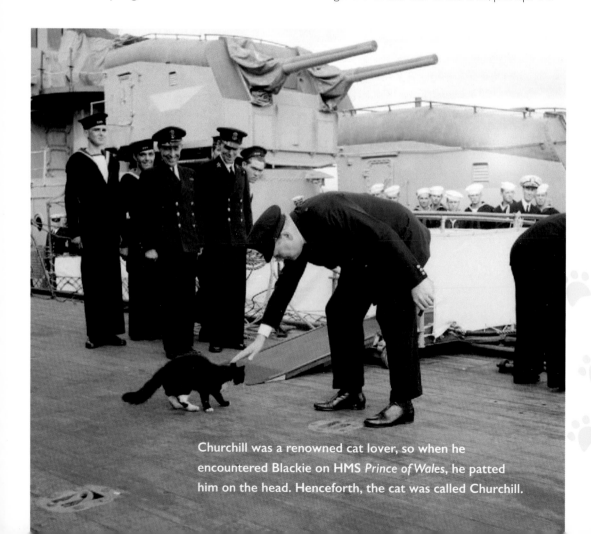

Churchill was a renowned cat lover, so when he encountered Blackie on HMS *Prince of Wales*, he patted him on the head. Henceforth, the cat was called Churchill.

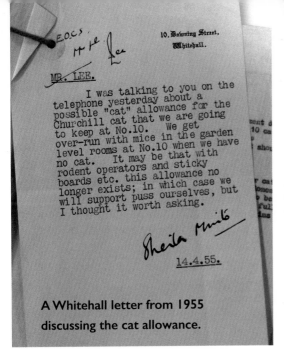

A Whitehall letter from 1955 discussing the cat allowance.

Jock VI is the current cat in residence at Chartwell, Winston Churchill's family home.

best contender was Jumbo, the War Cabinet Mouse Exterminator.

Jumbo's government career seems to have begun in 1936, when a Cabinet official requested an allowance from the Treasury for two cats, to deal with the mice that 'overran' the Cabinet Office.

By 1939 Jumbo needed a 'deputy'. The Cabinet Office had just reoccupied a building that Jumbo refused to patrol. An official lamented that Jumbo 'could not be induced to expand his sphere of action … being just a cat and therefore without any sense of gratitude towards the hand that feeds him'.

Jumbo died in 1942. He was missed and it was promised that his life would 'be recorded in the CAT-alogue of Events during the war'.

Jumbo needed a replacement and a female candidate was proposed. 'Her qualifications for the post are somewhat obscure,' her referee noted, 'but it is known that her enthusiasm and ability for increasing the feline population in this locality is very great.' She was accepted.

'Clemmie' (Clementine) Churchill – or 'Kat' – often drew pictures of a cat at the end of her letters to Winston, as seen here in a letter of 1909. Reproduced with permission of the Master and Fellows of Churchill College, Cambridge

The Official Home Office Cat

Larry, Palmerston and Gladstone are, without a doubt, pampered cats. Such is the adoration that they command that their every move is recorded for posterity. Historic mousers did not garner so much attention, so the records of their time in government are often scant.

The Home Office's official cats are exceptions to this rule. This great office of state recorded the lives of its mousers with meticulous and loving detail for more than half a century.

It all began in 1929, when the Treasury agreed to spend one pence a day for the upkeep of Peter, a black cat already resident in the Home Office. Peter's allowance was granted not because he was underfed; it was to stop him being overindulged by besotted civil servants. A near-constant stream of titbits had rendered Peter rather neglectful of his mouse-catching duties.

On his new diet, Peter hunted admirably. However, by November 1946 he was 17 and

Could this be Peter I outside Number 10 in 1938?

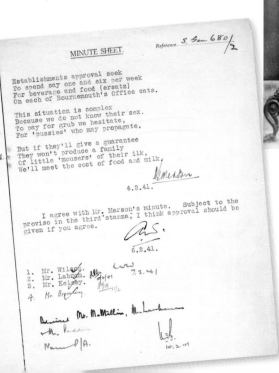

The Home Office responds poetically to requests for further cat allowances, 1941.

didn't meet the Treasury's requirement of an 'efficient cat'. He was replaced the next month by a kitten dubbed Peter II, who was sadly run over six months later.

Peter the Great

Peter II was succeeded in the role of official Home Office cat by (the imaginatively named) Peter III on 27 August 1947. Such was the Home Office's — and the nation's — affection for Peter III that perhaps he should have been called Peter the Great. In many ways he was Britain's first celebrity mouser.

It took a decade for Peter's star to ascend. In 1958 he appeared on BBC television's *Tonight* programme. A raft of newspaper and magazine appearances followed — Britain was smitten with the Home Office kitten.

Peter's celebrity brought his pay (still more or less what his predecessor got in 1929) to the public's attention. Many cat lovers and animal charities were incensed at his measly allowance, calling it starvation rations.

The Home Office were unmoved, though, coolly explaining that Peter was not overfed, thus ensuring his 'efficiency' as a mouser:

> The mice which Peter is employed to catch are not mere 'perks'; they are intended to be, and should be, his staple food … Peter's emoluments are not designed to keep him in food: if they were, they would also keep him in idleness.

The Home Office official sought to further calm cat lovers by noting that Peter had recently left a pigeon in his desk, observing that 'though chewed, it was not consumed, suggesting he is not suffering from starvation'.

Much of Peter III's National Archives file is made up of adoring correspondence from his admirers,

---

31st October, 1962.

ESG 499/1/1

Dear Miss Hargreaves,

Thank you for your letter to the Home Secretary about the office cat.

You will be pleased to know, I am sure, that Peter manages very well on the money the Treasury allows for his upkeep and his diet is supplemented, unofficially but very plentifully, by admirers who bring daily gifts of fish and meat.

Peter does not seem to have cat-friends; his recreations include pigeon fancying.

Yours sincerely,

Gary Davies,

Public Relations Branch.

A letter to a Miss Hargreaves in 1962 reassuring her that Peter's cat allowance was sufficient.

and the official replies give us an insight into Peter's daily life and character. Peter, it seems, was a solitary type with no known 'cat-friends'. He was, however, noted for his 'pigeon fancying', which suggests that more than one civil servant was given a feathery gift during Peter's tenure.

Peter III was put to sleep on 9 March 1964 and interred beneath a fine marble headstone in a pet cemetery. The Home Office received many letters of condolence from all over Britain and further afield, including one from the New York Transit Authority's 'Etti-Cat', a feline dedicated to promoting courtesy on the subway. A staggering number of letters also came from Italy, where Peter was clearly something of a celebrity!

It would be hard to disagree that, despite never officially holding the title Chief Mouser, Peter was, for his 17-year tenure, Whitehall's Top Cat.

Peta – DiploCAT Gone Wild

Peter was replaced in May 1964 by a pedigree black Manx cat named Manninagh Katedhu, a gift from the Isle of Man government. The Home Office renamed her Peta.

An official noted that Peta was from 'a diplomatic background'. Accordingly, she was to be paid an annual 'salary' of £13, more than double her predecessor's.

Peta received fan mail from all over the world, including adoring letters from children which have been preserved at The National Archives.

Home Office staff indulged Peta, plying her with treats – but these proved to be her undoing. By 1967 there were complaints that Peta was 'inordinately fat' and 'lazy in her habits'. She was also suspected of fighting with Prime Minister Harold Wilson's personal cat Nemo. Mary Wilson, the PM's wife, was injured trying to break up a catfight – the scratch on her arm meant she could not have the Italian Prime Minister for dinner!

Peta was sent away for 're-education' but didn't change her ways. In 1968 she was 'put out to grass' at a civil servant's rural home.

An internal memo dated 1964 concerning the replacement of Peter III with the Manx cat, Peta – a female.

FF - IN CONFIDENCE

Sir Charles Cunningham

1. Sir Charles Cunningham
2. Mr. Orton

I attach a note on the replacement for Peter, the cat.

I understand that it has been traditional for our cats to be (a) male and (b) named Peter: consequently the news that the replacement is to be a female sets us back a bit! However, we propose to call her Peta.

I gather she is likely to arrive in about a fortnight, the Manx Board of Agriculture using the intervening time to "house-train" her!

25th March, 1964.

For political as well as feline reasons, we must make sure Peta is happy with us.

HB.
26/3

The Admiralty Cat

In 1921 Britain was in dire financial straits. The Liberal–Conservative coalition government was seeking to economise wherever it could, particularly within the civil service. It appointed Sir Eric Geddes to chair a Committee of National Expenditure, tasked with seeking out waste and expelling it from the balance sheet. Sir Eric became known as the Geddes Axe.

Going against the culture of financial retrenchment in this period was the Admiralty (the government department in command of the Royal Navy), which called for one vital member of staff to receive a pay rise – the Office Cat.

In April 1921 Henry Scotten applied for an increased cat allowance. Since 1902 (and possibly before, no one quite knew) the cat had been provided for with an allowance of one shilling a week. But prices had gone up and Scotten requested an additional sixpence a week for the moggy.

Scotten's boss approved the request, but it also had to be considered by the Board of Admiralty. The culture of government parsimony might have been the reason for this escalation; however, like today it was probably done to encourage the circulation of cat jokes around the office.

Thankfully, Viscount Fareham, the First Lord and Head of the Board, seemed relaxed about the cat receiving a pay rise, but being a landlubber and politician he deferred to the experience of the professional navy, which had, he understood, 'a wide experience of seagoing cats and of the effect of victualling on their efficiency and morale'.

But not all of the First Lord's colleagues were quite so sanguine about the Admiralty Mouser's future. Ernle Chatfield, Assistant Chief of Naval Staff, noted that the cat might be obsolete as a weapon in combatting rodents, 'owing to the progress being made in Chemical Warfare'. Perhaps it should be considered 'whether this type of destroyer should not be placed on the disposal list', especially considering the 'high prices now obtaining in the fur trade'.

Fortunately, Chatfield was rebuffed by Leopold Amery MP, the Board's Secretary. Amery remarked that 'however attractive the use of poisonous gases may appear', their use inside the office might lead to a rapid increase in 'ex-members of Admiralty staff'. After all, you can't be poisoned by a cat; it just might fall asleep on your typewriter.

17-5-21

I hesitate to commit the Treasury to this increased charge without being assured of the support of those of my colleagues on the Board who are better qualified than I to judge of feline necessities. The Navy has, I understand, a wide experience of seagoing cats and of the effect of victualling on their efficiency and morale. The First Sea Lord has, moreover, commanded a Squadron of 'Cat' cruisers in action, and should be able to throw some light on the value, or otherwise, of the proposed charge. D.C.N.S. & A.C.N.S. might have something to add, from the staff point of view, on the more technical aspects of this mobile defence against rat raiders. Neither Second Sea Lord nor Controller appears to be specially concerned, but Fourth Sea Lord (subject always to financial considerations, which would require the concurrence of the Secretary) must obviously have the last word in a matter which is primarily one of Navy Victualling. All that I insist on is that, whatever decision is come to, it must

Tiddles, of HMS *Victorious*, at his favourite station on the after capstan, July 1942. © IWM

Royal Navy Ships' Cats

Beyond the offices of the Admiralty itself, the Royal Navy's fleet has played host to countless brave military moggies over the years. Cats were banned by the navy for hygiene reasons in 1975, but before that many ship's mousers had served with distinction, including in wartime.

In 1906 the Royal Navy revolutionised naval warfare by launching HMS *Dreadnought*, a floating fortress capable of high speeds and armed to the teeth with massive artillery pieces. Modernity was the *Dreadnought*'s watchword, but one all-important feature was as old as seafaring itself: the ship's cat. *Dreadnought*'s mascot Togo liked to relax in the barrels of the ship's giant guns!

There are many other notable maritime moggies; for example,

HMS *Hermione*'s cat Convoy so delighted his shipmates that they made him a cat-sized hammock – for comfortable catnapping. Sea cat Tiddles, meanwhile, has the distinction of being one of the navy's best-travelled felines. In the 1940s Tiddles served on the aircraft carriers *Argus* and *Victorious*. In the course of his voyages he clocked up over 30,000 sea miles – truly a cat of the world.

Able Seaman Simon, the Navy's Most Decorated Cat

Although many naval cats have been celebrated, few have been decorated. One exception is 'Able Seaman' Simon, the cat of HMS *Amethyst*.

In 1949 the Chinese civil war was raging between Communist and Nationalist forces. The *Amethyst* had been sent up the Yangtze River to guard the British Embassy. However, on 20 April the *Amethyst* was shelled by Communist forces and ran aground. The ship remained stuck and under attack for three months before it managed to escape.

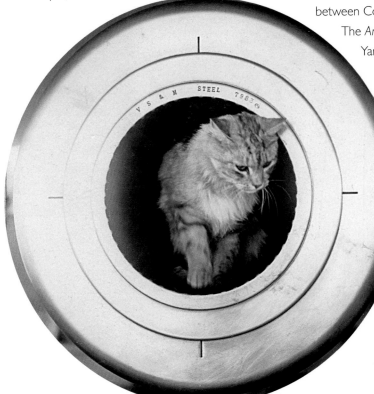

Togo on HMS Dreadnought.

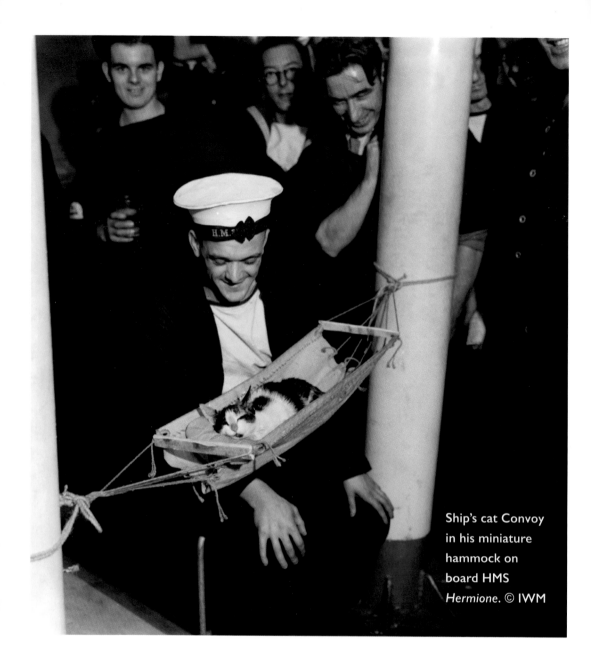

Ship's cat Convoy in his miniature hammock on board HMS *Hermione*. © IWM

The Amethyst Incident was an international scandal, and the crew became heroes honoured by the nation. This included the ship's cat Simon.

Simon, it transpired, had been injured during the initial shelling of the ship. Undeterred, he had disregarded his wounds and continued to deal with the ship's rat infestation – vital work when food supplies were dwindling.

With the *Amethyst* back at port, Simon was recommended for the Our Dumb Friends League Blue Cross medal. He also received the People's Dispensary for Sick Animals Dickin Medal – the highest honour a military animal can receive. Simon remains the Dickin's only feline recipient.

Simon, of HMS *Amethyst*, with his Dickin Medal.

Cats on board the cruiser HMS *Hawkins*.

Mousers Save the Mail

Anyone who has had the misfortune of suffering a domestic mouse infestation will know that those pesky rodents are a direct threat to a household's food supply; every strand of spaghetti, every grain of rice, every crust of bread is under threat.

But if you think that's bad, imagine a time when mice and rats threatened your bank balance. This is a problem that the Post Office had to contend with in the 19th century.

In 1868 a Post Office official from one of London's central sorting offices wrote to his superiors about the destruction mice and rats were wreaking on the mail – and, more worryingly, on money orders. Rodents were gnawing away at the country's financial security.

Traps had been of no use, the frustrated postie reported, but there was one solution – a cat.

Three moggies were procured and an upkeep allowance was authorised.

The mousers were industrious. Nine months on it was noted 'that the cats have done their duty very efficiently'. Buoyed by this success, the employment of cats in post offices across the nation was approved.

The Post Office was determined to get mice for its money and instituted a system of periodic 'cat efficiency reports'. One memo sternly cautions that 'it is important that the cats be not overfed; they must depend on mice for the remainder of their emoluments'.

Most mousers seemed to have been up to muster. Nevertheless, their wages stagnated from about 1918 onwards. The situation became so

Below: **Victorian children post a letter, *c.*1895.**

Tibs the Great is no more

TIBS, the Post Office's number one cat, the imposing 23lb. giant who has reigned at Post Office Headquarters for 14 years, is no more.

Mr. Alf Talbut, Cleaner at St. Martin's-le-Grand, who has served his "Tibby" since the cat was born, never failing to come in at every Bank Holiday to see him fed, first realised something was wrong when Tibs failed to turn up for his morning meal one Monday just before Christmas. Reports came in that he had been seen on the floor above his basement home. Mr. Talbut began to leave food at strategic places and a little of it would go, but the big cat was not found until later in the week.

Mr. Talbut needed the help of a colleague to carry Tibs to the People's Dispensary for Sick Animals, where the veterinary surgeon was in no doubt. Tibs had cancer of the mouth. Almost exactly on his 14th birthday the life of the Post Office's senior cat was brought to a close.

Tibs was an official member of the Post Office staff and was paid 2s. 6d. a week. He lived in the basement and all his life he never ventured from the precincts of his domain—where no rat has been seen since Tibs sorted them out early in his career. (He once brought a pigeon into the basement. It was freed, shaken but unhurt.)

Twice Mr. Talbut took him from Headquarters. The first time was to the PDSA where he was detained for six weeks for treatment of an infected ear. When he was returned home fit and well, a collecting box for the PDSA

Tibs in 1954, as he appeared in the book Cockney Cats.

raised more than £50 from grateful members of the staff at Headquarters.

His second outing was to a special cats' and film stars' party, where Tibs was the dominant figure among the cream of the cat world.

There is no record of Tibs ever granting audience to a Postmaster General, but his fame had spread to nearby St. Bartholomew's Hospital where members of the staff often brought friends to "see for themselves."

"I looked after his mother, Minnie," said Mr. Talbut "she was a fine cat too, but Tibs was a worthy successor. I don't think we'll have another cat. There will never be another Tibs."

The obituary of Tibs the Great. © Royal Mail Group Ltd 1965, courtesy of The Postal Museum

A stamp printed in Great Britain for the 150th Anniversary of the Royal Society for the Prevention of Cruelty to Animals, 1990.

---

serious that questions were asked in the House of Commons in 1953. David Gammans, Assistant Post Master General, admitted to the scandalous feline pay freeze. He added that performance-related pay had proved impossible, owing to these feline employees being 'frequently unreliable, capricious in their duties and liable to prolonged absenteeism'.

No pay rise was forthcoming, which might have upset the Post Office's most famous mouser – Tibs the Great.

Tibs, who served from 1950 until 1964, was a giant of the cat world, weighing an astounding 23lb! Tibs's fame spread beyond the Post Office – in the 1960s he attended a 'cats and film stars party', hobnobbing with the 'cream of the cat world'.

The Post Office no longer keeps mousers on its staff, but Tibs the Great will long be fondly remembered.

1840 · RSPCA · 1990

A Paw-sitive Future

'One cat just leads to another.'

Ernest Hemingway

Cats are clearly back in vogue in Westminster. There has never been a better time to be a mouser it seems; rolling online news has made our appetite for updates on Larry and co. insatiable. These mousers are probably better known (and loved) than many of their human colleagues in the Cabinet.

They are the latest in a long and prestigious line of government tabbies. And while these modern moggies might not always be 'efficient mousers' by their feline forebears' exacting standards, they perform their other, arguably more vital, role with the same grace as their predecessors – to delight civil servants, politicians and the public.

While wars raged, markets collapsed and governments crumbled, these 'official' felines were there to lift their human co-workers' spirits. They are a testament to the enduring affection humans – and even civil servants – have for cats.

Artificial pest control methods have improved since the 19th century, but it seems unlikely we will see the end of Official Mousers. After all, these furry functionaries don't just keep the corridors of power free of mice; they fill them with joy, too.